ST

DISCARD

DINOSAURS
OPPOSING VIEWPOINTS®

Look for these and other exciting *Great Mysteries:*

The Bermuda Triangle
Dinosaurs
Poltergeists
Pyramids
The Solar System
Witches

GREAT MYSTERIES

DINOSAURS
OPPOSING VIEWPOINTS®

PETER & CONNIE ROOP

Central Rappahannock Regional Library
1201 Caroline Street
Fredericksburg, VA. 22401

Greenhaven Press, Inc.   San Diego, California

No part of this book may be reproduced or used in any form or by any means, electrical, mechanical, or otherwise, including, but not limited to photocopy, recording, or any information storage and retrieval system, without prior written permission from the publisher.

Book design by Joan Gordon, Minneapolis
Cover design by FAB Artists, Minneapolis

Library of Congress Cataloging-in-Publication Data

Roop, Peter.
    Dinosaurs : opposing viewpoint.

    (Great mysteries)
    Bibliography: p.
    Includes index.
    Summary: Discusses possible reasons for the extinction of the dinosaurs.
    1. Dinosaurs—Juvenile literature. [1. Dinosaurs]
I. Roop, Connie. II. Title. III. Series: Great mysteries (Saint Paul, Minn.)
QE862.D5R64   1987   567.9'1   87-7516
ISBN 0-89908-050-2 (lib. bdg.)

© Copyright 1988 Greenhaven Press, Inc.
Every effort has been made to trace owners of copyright material.

For Peter Betzer whose enthusiasm for scientific inquiry inspires us.

Contents

	Introduction	9
1	Prehistoric Death	10
2	Mammals vs. Dinosaurs	30
3	Climate as Killer	46
4	Cosmic Collision	60
5	More Heavenly Theories	74
	The Search Goes On...	86
	Books for Further Exploration	89
	Glossary	90
	Index	93
	About the Authors	95

"We have . . . searched under the junipers for some dinosaur bones and come face to face with ourselves."
John Noble Wilford, *The Riddle of the Dinosaur*

Introduction

"Penetrating so many secrets, we cease to believe in the unknowable. But there it sits nevertheless, calmly licking its chops."

H.L. Mencken, American essayist

This book is written for the curious—those who enjoy the hunt for possible solutions to the unexplained.

Mysteries are everywhere. To be human is to be constantly surrounded by wonderment. How do birds fly? Are ghosts real? How sophisticated is animal communication? How did the first baker discover how to make bread? Why are there no more dodo birds? Was King Arthur real or a fiction? Where did the world come from? Where is it going?

Great Mysteries: Opposing Viewpoints books are intended to offer the reader an opportunity to explore some of the many mysteries that both trouble and intrigue us. For the span of each book, we want the reader to feel that he or she *is* a scientist exploring the extinction of the dinosaur, an archaeologist exploring the origins of the great Egyptian pyramids, a psychic detective exploring the existence of magic.

One thing all mysteries have in common is that there is no ready answer. Often there are *many* answers but none on which even the majority of authorities agrees. *Great Mysteries: Opposing Viewpoints* books introduce the intriguing views of the experts, allowing the reader to participate in their explorations, their theories, and their disagreements as they try to explain the mysteries of our world.

But most readers won't want to stop here. *Great Mysteries: Opposing Viewpoints* aim to stimulate the reader's curiosity. Although truth is often impossible to discover, the search is fascinating. It is up to the reader to examine the evidence, to decide whether the answer is there—or to explore further.

One

A Prehistoric Death

Sixty-five million years ago, a herd of hungry *Triceratops* browsed through a forest. The shade beneath the trees brought relief from the searing midday sun. The animals lumbered on toward the cooling waters of a pond. One of the *Triceratops* stopped for a mouthful of leaves. Glancing up, it saw a brilliant light streaking toward the earth. The *Triceratops* paid no attention to this "second sun."

Within seconds the herd lay dead. They had been killed by the shock waves that a burning asteroid created as it crashed into earth. The impact levelled forests for hundreds of miles. Huge clouds of rock and ash rocketed skyward. The sun grew dim through the ever-increasing cloud of debris hurled up by the impact of the asteroid.

The heavy, dark cloud spread to fill the sky. Within weeks, sunlight was cut off from large portions of the earth's surface. Plants wilted and died. Many of the browsing

animals, dinosaurs and mammals alike, died of starvation. Plankton in the sea, the primary food source from marine life, vanished as the sunlight disappeared. Death and desolation reigned over the earth. Only a few hardy plants, reptiles, and mammals survived the catastrophe.

No dinosaur survived. Never again would these once-plentiful animals roam the earth. All were extinct.

Mysterious Extinction

This is only one scenario scientists imagine in their continuing effort to solve a great mystery: What happened to the dinosaurs? Did they die in the fiery impact of an asteroid, or did a supernova, an exceedingly bright star, explode nearby and radiate them to extinction? Did an expanding mammal population hasten their end by eating too many dinosaur eggs, or did a gradual cooling of the earth cause the dinosaurs to disappear forever?

> *Indeed, the death of the dinosaurs is the single greatest mystery in paleontology, and one of the most compelling mysteries in all of science."*
> *Author Daniel Cohen,* Monster Dinosaur

For over 150 years scientists and lay people alike have tried to discover what caused the death of the dinosaurs. Proposed answers range from the unlikely suggestion of drug addiction to more plausible scientific theories such as the impact of an asteroid. Today the reason for the disappearance of dinosaurs remains a mystery. While much evidence has been discovered, no theory has been universally accepted. More clues may be hidden beneath the earth's surface or in the vastness of outer space.

Amazingly, this compelling mystery wasn't even discovered until the early 1800s. Before then, there was no mystery to solve; no one had even heard of a dinosaur.

Dr. Gideon Mantell is credited with the first dinosaur discovery. Dr. Mantell, an English country doctor, had a keen interest in fossils. He continually collected them, even as he

Dr. Gideon Mantell, who, with his wife Mary, discovered and named the first dinosaur teeth.

made his rounds to patients. Mary, his wife, often accompanied him on his rounds. It was actually she who made the first major contribution to our knowledge of dinosaurs.

One day in 1822, while waiting outside a patient's home in southern England, Mary picked up a large tooth in the gravel on the road. Knowing her husband would be interested, she kept the tooth to show him. Pleased and excited by her discovery, Dr. Mantell set out to find where the gravel had been quarried. Upon locating the source, he soon found other examples of these teeth, the likes of which he had never seen before.

> "Maybe there just wasn't room for them on the ark!"
>
> *Physicist Richard Muller, University of California Berkeley*

Dr. Mantell studied the strange teeth, asked his fellow fossil collectors about them, and even sent one to the Baron Georges Cuvier, one of the most respected scientists of that time. After examining the samples, Cuvier declared them to be rhinoceros teeth.

But Gideon Mantell remained puzzled. To him they did not seem like rhinoceros teeth.

Then, while comparing one of the gigantic teeth with

Tooth identified by Dr. Mantell as belonging to a creature previously unknown.

others in a museum's fossil collection, Dr. Mantell examined the tooth of an iguana. The two teeth, one large, the other tiny, were virtually identical. Because of the similarity of the two teeth, Mantell named his fossil *Iguanodon*, which means "iguana-tooth."

The Evidence Multiplies

As news of Mantell's discovery spread, more unusual teeth and bones came to light. Identification of each specimen was attempted. Evidence mounted that some remarkable animals had once lived throughout England, animals unlike any still known to exist in the nineteenth century.

By 1842, so many fossil specimens had been collected that a new word was needed to describe these extinct lizardlike animals. The preeminent British scientist Sir

Fossilized dinosaur skin.

Richard Owen combined the two Greek words *deinos* ("terrible") and *sauros* ("lizards") to create a new word, *"Dinosauria."*

Discoveries about dinosaurs have continued since Dr. Mantell's time, giving us a fairly accurate picture of them and their world. Yet despite many museum collections of dinosaur fossils, scientists remain uncertain why these animals perished.

The Fossil Record

Our entire knowledge of dinosaurs comes from the fossil record—those few bones, teeth, and footprints of the once-living creatures that have been preserved through time. By examining fossil clues, scientists have gradually pieced together many parts of the puzzle of dinosaur life.

A fossil is any evidence of ancient plant or animal life preserved in rock or sediment. Most typically the hard parts of an animal (shells, bones, or teeth) are fossilized. Only rarely do soft materials like feathers or skin leave a fossil imprint. Given the right conditions, however, even a

Technician carefully examining and cleaning fossils.

15

Fossilized dinosaur footprints in Texas.

footprint can become fossilized. Fossils can be dinosaur footprints hardened in shale, insects preserved in amber (fossilized tree resin), oyster shells in limestone, mineralized bones and teeth, imprints of fern leaves in coal, or pieces of petrified wood. Occasionally an entire fossilized animal skeleton is discovered. The most common fossils are of marine life—an imprint of a shell in rock, for example.

Paleontologists, scientists who study fossils, examine life forms found in the rocks. They have discovered evidence that living organisms existed on earth at least two and a half billion years ago. But relatively few specimens of all the plants and animals that have lived on earth remain as fossils. Why? Because the earth is dynamic and changing, and because the process of fossilization is dependent upon certain conditions.

The earth's surface has been continually reshaped since the planet first formed some 4.5 billion years ago. Wind and water weather away mountains, volcanic eruptions build new landforms or cover existing ones, entire continents break up and drift slowly over the globe, seabeds lift up and warp to become mountain ranges, oceans rise and fall. To us the

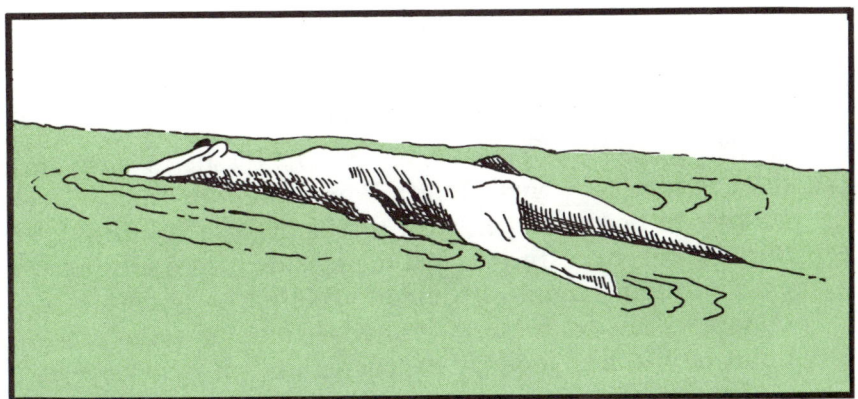
After an animal dies, dirt, sand, and debris begin to cover its body.

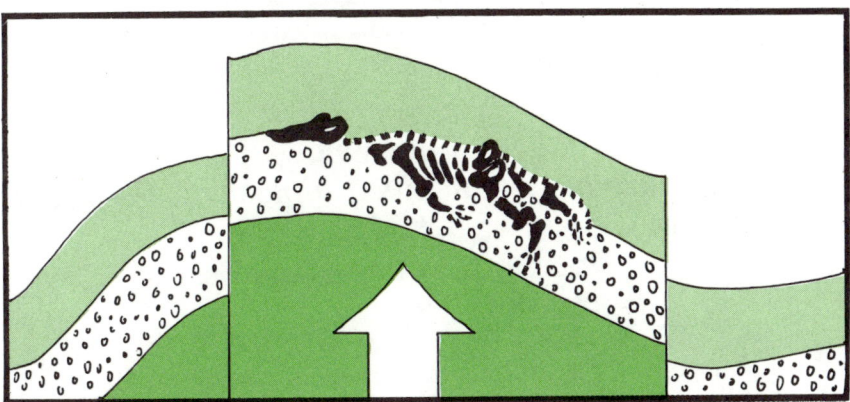
As the body decays, the dirt layers increase. The mud and sand harden and become rock; minerals petrify the animal's remains. Over time, the earth and rock layers shift dramatically.

Eventually, erosion wears away the rock layers, exposing the fossil.

changes seem imperceptibly slow. Yet in the vastness of geologic time, they occur in dramatically small periods of time.

A *Triceratops* Becomes a Fossil

The conditions necessary for most fossils to form make the chances very small that a bone, tooth, or footprint will survive to become one. Most fossils are the result of rapid burial in an undisturbed sediment, slow decomposition, and gradual replacement of their internal parts by certain minerals. Once a fossil is formed, it must survive erosion, uplift, and other geologic processes until it is discovered.

Imagine two *Triceratops* that die at the same time. One is killed and eaten by a *Tyrannosaurus rex*. Hungry scavengers devour what the tyrannosaur leaves behind. Once the flesh is gone, the bones slowly dissolve, leaving no evidence of the dinosaur's existence.

> "The problem is not what killed the dinosaurs but what killed almost all the life at the time."
>
> *Physicist Luis Alvarez, University of California, Berkeley*

The other *Triceratops*, however, is unexpectedly overwhelmed by a flash flood. Crushed beneath a flow of mud and debris, the entire dinosaur is protected from predators and from rapid disintegration by bacteria. Over thousands of years, more sediment is deposited upon the mudflow. Compressed by the weight of these deposits, the mud is gradually changed into shale.

During this time of deposition and compression, the dinosaur skeleton fossilizes. The soft parts dissolve. They are gradually replaced by minerals from water. The minerals become an exact replica of the original bones.

For millions of years, the fossilized bones remain buried beneath the earth's surface. During this time, however, the shale is slowly uplifted. As the land rises, a river cuts its bed deeper and deeper into the rock. Wind and water wear away the rock until the dinosaur skeleton is exposed. Obviously, only a very small percentage of plant and animal remains will surmount the difficulties of fossilization; only a very small percentage will remain as specimens for the study of future generations.

Earth's Time Scale

To help us understand the history of the earth, geologists, or earth scientists, have created a time scale. This scale breaks down the 4.5 billion years of earth's history into distinct units. The units are identified by the types of rock found at various levels and by the fossils found in them. Certain plants and animals lived at specific times. Their fossils help geologists date the earth. The geologic time scale has four major eras: the Precambrian, meaning "before life"; the Paleozoic, "old life"; the Mesozoic, "middle life"; and the Cenozoic, "recent life." These major blocks of time are further broken down into units called periods.

Geologic time is immense. If earth's 4.5 billion years were compressed into a single year, the Precambrian era would extend from January into May, during which primitive plants like algae would evolve. The Paleozoic era would extend from May to early December when corals, fish, amphibians, and land plants develop. Dinosaurs, in the Mesozoic era, would be the dominant form of life by mid-December and would become extinct by December 26. Humanlike animals, evolving during the Cenozoic era, would appear on this year-long calendar on the evening of December 31 with the Declaration of Independence being signed seven-tenths of a second before midnight!

> *The mystery of the catastrophe at the end of the Cretaceous is not so much why many died off, but why any survived at all."*
> Geologist Kenneth J. Hsu, The Great Dying

The Mesozoic era, often called the Age of Reptiles, extended from 225 million years ago to 65 million years ago. This is the time when dinosaurs roamed the earth. The Mesozoic era includes three periods called the Triassic, Jurassic, and Cretaceous. Dinosaurs reached their peak

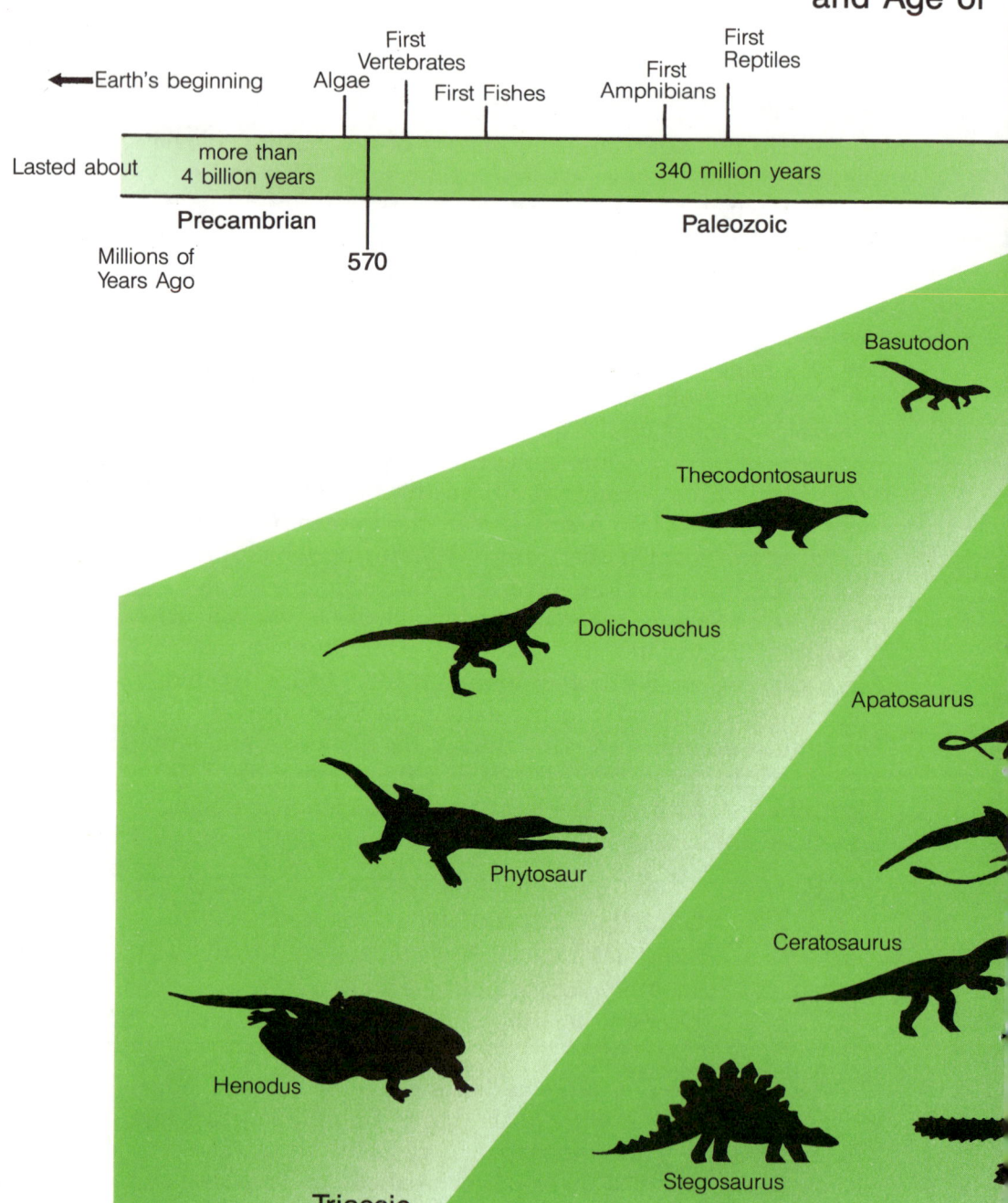

Time Scale
the Dinosaurs

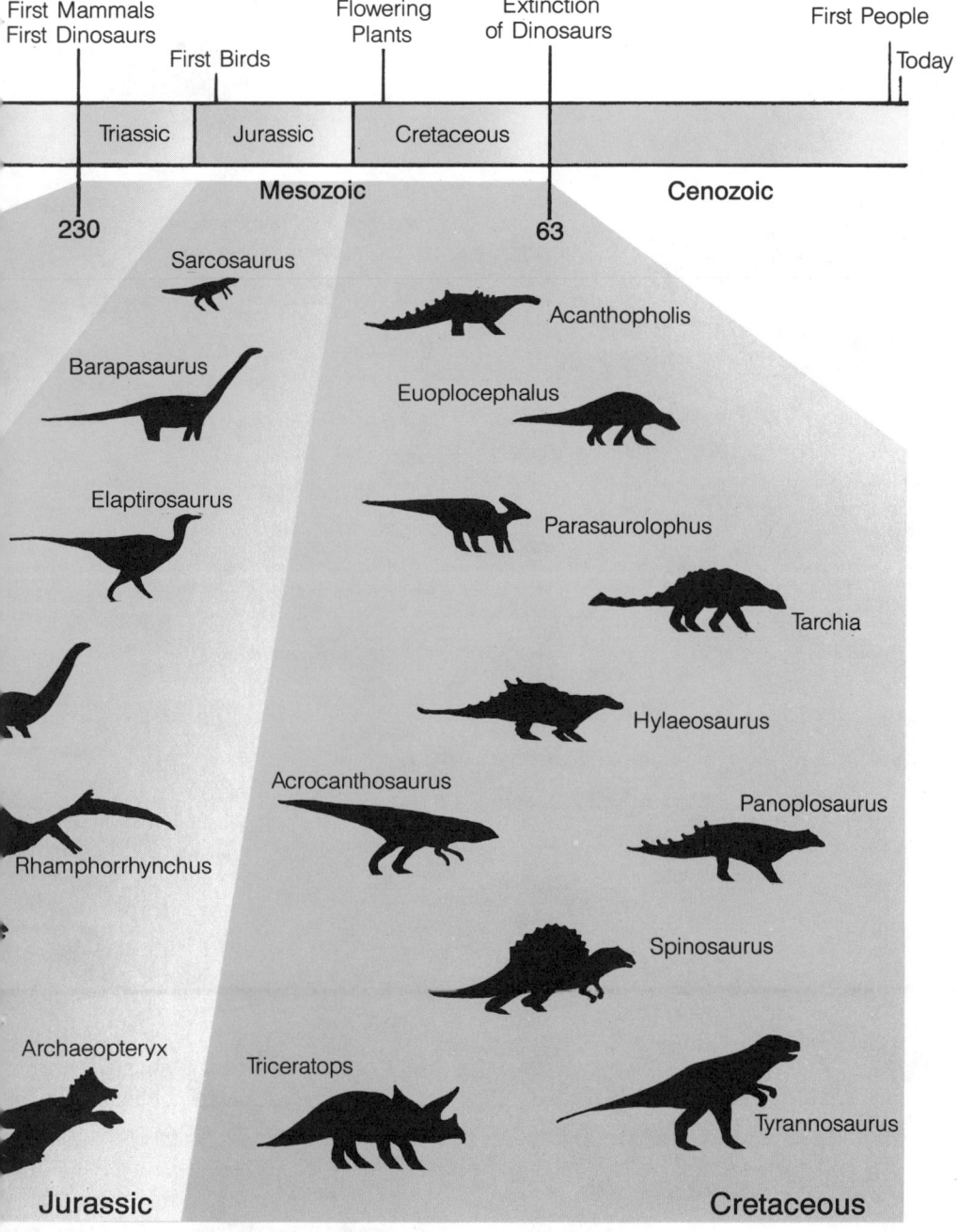

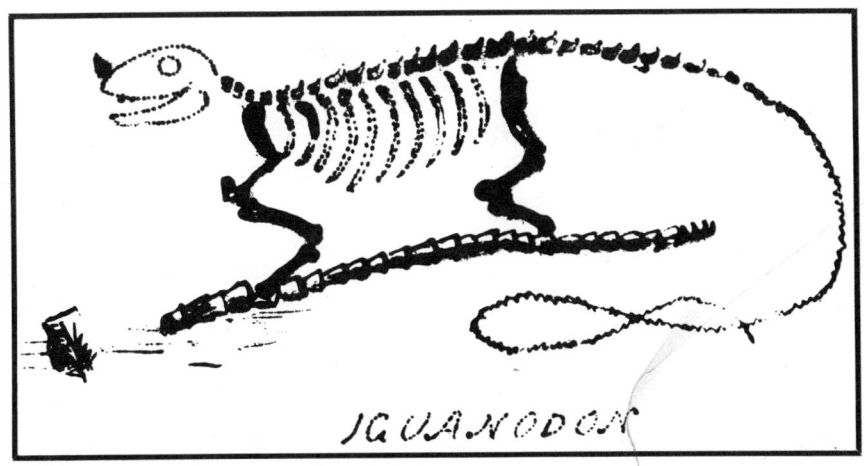

Above is a drawing of an *Iquanodon* as imagined in the time of Dr. Gideon Mantell. On the left is a recent drawing of an *Iquanodon*. The addition of more evidence and more detailed study has drastically altered scientists' views.

during the Jurassic period.

A tremendous variety of dinosaurs lived in what is now North America. Large *Brachiosaurus, Diplodocus,* and *Apatosaurus* (often called *Brontosaurus*) browsed on the lush tropical vegetation. These four-legged herbivores, or plant eaters, long-necked, and long-tailed, consumed vast amounts of foliage to sustain their massive bodies. Some weighed as much as eighty tons and grew to ninety feet in length. Many smaller plant-eating dinosaurs shared the lowland areas with these Jurassic giants. *Camptosaurus* grew up to fifteen feet in length. It could walk on all fours but usually was bipedal, walking on its hind limbs. *Stegosaurus*, with its spiked tail and triangular plates down the spine, feasted on vegetation, too. It walked on four feet and grew to a length of twenty feet.

Carnivores, or meat eaters, were as varied in size as the herbivores. The largest of the carnivores during the Jurassic period was *Allosaurus*. *Allosaurus* swiftly crossed the landscape on its two strong hind legs. Grasping its prey with small, clawed forelimbs, it ripped apart and ate both large and small herbivores with its dagger-sharp teeth and massive jaws. Teeth marks that match the spacing of *Allosaurus* teeth have been found in fossil vertebrae of *Apatosaurus*.

> **"***The real reasons for the dinosaur extinctions have to do with temperature and sea-level changes, the spread of diseases by migration and other complex events."*
>
> *Robert T. Bakker, University of Colorado Museum*

Allosaurus was the evolutionary predecessor of the famous and largest carnivorous dinosaur, *Tyrannosaurus rex*.

Much smaller was *Ornitholestes*, which was about six feet long and stood on its hind legs like *Allosaurus*. Its claws were arranged for grasping small prey like lizards. The smallest flesh-eating dinosaur was *Compsognathus*. It was about the size of a chicken and also ate lizards. One fossil specimen of this dinosaur was found with a lizard skeleton within its body cavity.

The World of the Dinosaurs

What was the world of the dinosaurs like? Was it similar to ours or vastly different? In fact it was both, since the earth changed dramatically during the days of the dinosaurs. The first dinosaurs in the Upper Triassic period lived in a world very different from ours. But by the time dinosaurs died out, the earth was much as we know it.

The earliest dinosaurs lived in a much less complex

Four stages in the transition from a single continent—Pangaea—to today's

> *"You can have an organism that's perfectly adapted to its environment and then — whappo—along comes a meteor or a mammoth volcanic eruption."*
>
> Professor David Clark, University of Wisconsin

environment. Where there are now seven distinct continents, there was then only one, which geologists call Pangaea. One unbroken ocean surrounded this supercontinent.

Over millions of years, Pangaea broke into two parts, Laurasia and Gondwanaland. Later these two supercontinents split, and the separated landmasses gradually drifted to their present locations. Such continental movement continues even today. North America, for example, is moving away from Europe at the rate of one inch a year.

The land itself was relatively flat during the days of the first dinosaurs. Low, small hills covered the landscape. No great mountain ranges rose to the sky. Today's Himalaya and Rocky Mountains began to form only in the final stages of the Cretaceous period. Dinosaurs, unhindered by steep elevations, could roam where they wished.

The early dinosaurs enjoyed a warmer, more temperate climate than is found in most parts of the world today. The climate of the Mesozoic era was like the tropical and near-tropical climates found today in the Amazon River basin and

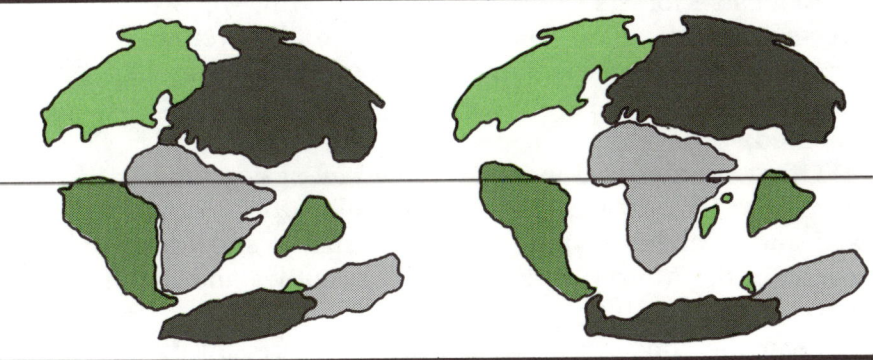

multiple continents. Scientists say the land masses are continuing to move.

Florida. The climate was remarkably similar throughout the world. There was plenty of rain and no snow. The poles were free of ice.

Extensive forests flourished in this warm, wet world. Tree-sized ferns, giant conifers, and palmlike cycads covered the rolling hills and low-lying swamps. Open savannahs stretched for miles. No grasses yet grew; no flowers bloomed.

Other reptiles and mammals lived alongside the dinosaurs. Lizards and fifty-foot-long alligators roamed the land and swamps. Flying reptiles the size of small airplanes soared in the Mesozoic skies. Smaller reptiles and mammals scurried through the underbrush.

Over the eons during which the dinosaurs lived, the world changed drastically. The continents separated and moved. Flowering plants emerged and spread. Different

Scientists and other important men having dinner in a reconstruction of an *Iquanodon* in England, 1854. As more and more information about dinosaurs became available, this model was discovered to be far from realistic.

types of trees like oaks and poplars developed. Marine animals like bony fish evolved.

As the world changed, so did dinosaurs. As with all life forms, some dinosaur species died out while new ones appeared. For example, the large, plated dinosaur *Stegosaurus* became extinct at the beginning of the Cretaceous period. *Triceratops*, on the other hand, did not begin to inhabit the land until after *Stegosaurus* was extinct. *Tyrannosaurus* lived in the Cretaceous period; *Apatosaurus* lived in both the Jurassic and Cretaceous periods. Several hundred species of dinosaurs evolved and adapted to changing living conditions throughout the millions of years called the Age of Reptiles.

Humanlike creatures have populated the earth for less than 4 million years. In comparison, the dinosaurs inhabited the earth for about 150 million years. Dinosaurs varied tremendously in form and size just as mammals do today.

Modern mammals include the 100-ton blue whale and the 5-ounce mole; dinosaurs ranged in size from the chicken-sized *Compsognathus* to the 100-ton *Seismosaurus*. Some dinosaurs were herbivores; others were carnivores. Some moved slowly; others swiftly attacked fleeing prey.

Fossil evidence shows that the dinosaurs disappeared between the Mesozoic and Cenozoic eras. Their extinction may seem abrupt. But, although it could have happened in less than a decade, the process may actually have taken hundreds of thousands of years. The geologic time scale covers millions of years, and geologic processes occur slowly. Mountains are eroded away grain by grain. Centuries must pass before any significant changes in the rock record appear.

> *"Debate . . . is the engine of scientific advancement, and there is every reason to think that one of the greatest mysteries in the history of life is lurching toward a solution."*
> Writer Boyce Rensberger, Science Digest, May 1986

Fossil evidence makes one thing clear, though. Dinosaurs were not the only life forms to vanish at this time. Some seventy percent of life then on earth disappeared—the majority of microscopic animals, all the pterosaurs (flying reptiles), the icthyosaurs and plesiosaurs (large marine animals), the mosasaurs (marine lizards), and numerous plants.

What killed them? Why did so many life forms die out while others, like crocodiles, turtles, snakes, horseshoe crabs, and ginkgo trees, continued to live and flourish? The fact that not all life forms perished along with the dinosaurs complicates the mystery.

Two

Mammals vs. Dinosaurs

For years many scientists believed that mammals were the culprits who did in the dinosaurs. After all, didn't many mammals live on after the dinosaurs died? Why did mammals survive when the dinosaurs did not?

Mammals vs. Dinosaurs

The basic premise in the theory of mammals vs. dinosaurs is that the comparatively small, agile mammals had a great taste for dinosaur eggs. From the study of fossils, we know that whereas some dinosaurs gave birth to live young, most laid eggs. Dinosaurs apparently did not hatch their eggs in safe, warm nests the way today's birds do. Instead, most egg-laying dinosaurs acted in much the same way as green turtles do today. They dug shallow pits, laid their eggs in them, covered them with dirt or sand, and left.

Fossilized nest of *Protoceratops* eggs. Nests like these are remarkably similar to nests made today by turtles—arranged in a circle and warmly protected by sand and other matter.

Mammals could have easily discovered the unguarded pits and feasted upon the eggs. The theory suggests that they did just that, eating so many eggs that few baby dinosaurs hatched to mature, mate, and bear young.

Even the few baby dinosaurs that hatched would have been in peril, according to the theory. When they emerged from their shells, they had to fend for themselves.

Yet could mammals have eaten enough eggs to have wiped out the dinosaurs? Many scientists today do not think so. For one thing, the mammals of the Cretaceous period were quite small compared to mammals of today. Most were the size of rats and lived on insects and seeds. In addition, mammals became numerous only after the dinosaurs disappeared. There just weren't enough large, egg-eating mammals around to have destroyed the numerous dinosaur species. Furthermore, mammals and dinosaurs lived side by side for millions of years, and dinosaurs remained the dominant life form throughout that period. It seems highly unlikely that after so many years of relatively peaceful coexistence, mammals would suddenly take such an interest in dinosaur eggs.

Perhaps the strongest argument against the egg-eating theory becomes obvious when we look at some of the other extinctions that took place at the time the dinosaurs became extinct. Not only did the dinosaurs die out; so did many plants, marine reptiles, and plankton. Egg-eating mammals could hardly be blamed for those deaths.

Dr. Stephen Jay Gould of Harvard University states, "To guess that dinosaurs died because small animals ate their eggs . . . is perennial untestable speculation."

Food Fight

Another theory pitting mammals against dinosaurs (and claiming mammal victory) states that mammals won in the battle for food. Fossil records, however, do not support this hypothesis. In fact, the study of fossils shows the opposite. Although mammal-like reptiles dominated the land in the

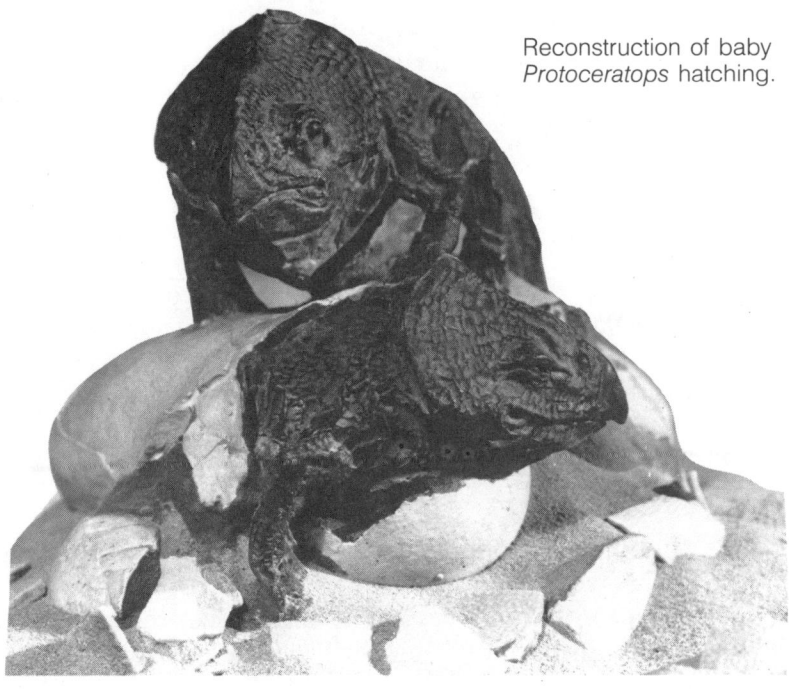

Reconstruction of baby *Protoceratops* hatching.

Permian and early Triassic periods (290-225 million years ago), they were themselves replaced by dinosaurs. The dinosaurs evolved into the dominant land animals, and mammals remained a relatively small group. While possibly eating some of the same foods as dinosaurs, mammals were too few and too small to compete successfully with them. The mammals came to the forefront only after the dinosaurs became extinct.

The mammals vs. dinosaurs theories may gain much of their popularity because we ourselves are mammals. Agile and intelligent, egg-eaters as well, we imaginatively transfer these traits to early mammals and see these skills as ones the dinosaurs lacked. Fossil records, however, do not support our imaginations. Dinosaurs came in an enormous variety of sizes and body structures. Many were extremely agile and probably enjoyed snacking on a mammal now and then.

Mini Brains

Several theories about dinosaur extinction claim that the dinosaurs' own physical flaws were the cause of their demise. One such theory is based on the small size of dinosaur brains in comparison to the size of their bodies. For example, the huge *Brontosaurus* (more recently scientifically named *Apatosaurus*) weighed forty-five tons but had a brain only the size of a grapefruit. Other dinosaurs also had small brains—some of the smallest in proportion to their bodies of all known vertebrates. Thus, states this theory, the dinosaurs were simply too stupid to adapt to changes in their world.

> *As wondrous as they were, the dinosaurs were limited. They were incapable of causing their own extinction."*
> Writer John Noble Wilford, The Riddle of the Dinosaurs

How then, argue opposing scientists, did they manage to adapt and survive the many changes the earth underwent during their 140-million-year reign? Brain size, these scientists maintain, is not necessarily a fair measurement of ability.

> *Dinosaurs weren't failures. They were extremely successful animals in charge of the land for 135 million years—more than twice as long as the mammals have been in control."*
> Paleontologist Robert T. Bakker, University of Colorado Museum

Once again we are forced to look at the other species that died out at the same time the dinosaurs became extinct. As Helen Sattler writes in her acclaimed book *Dinosaurs of North America*, "Stupidity couldn't have caused the plants and plankton to become extinct."

Clearly, the brain-size theory has its problems.

A similar theory proposes the dinosaurs were too big and clumsy to survive. Not too big and clumsy to survive 140 million years, just too big and clumsy to survive 150 million years? This theory too has its problems. When we study the fossils of some of these "clumsy" dinosaurs, we find that they were incredibly fast and agile. Take, for example, such dinosaurs as *Struthiomimus* and *Dromoaeosaurus*. *Struthiomimus* ("ostrich mimic") sprinted swiftly on its slim legs. It had keen eyes and long, slender, claw-tipped fingers. *Dromoaeosaurus* ("emu mimic") was probably the fastest dinosaur of all. Its lightweight body enabled it to run faster than a modern horse. Obviously, not *all* dinosaurs were slow and clumsy.

Death from Old Age

Some paleontologists have suggested that the dinosaurs as a species simply grew too old to continue and hence died out. These scientists argue that just as individuals go through

predictable life cycles (being born, maturing, dying), so do entire species. Maybe a species' ability to adapt to change wears out, just as some human beings lose their hearing as they age.

Other scientists argue that an entire species cannot be compared with individuals. A species, they say, does not have a pre-established life expectancy. Crocodiles, sharks, and horseshoe crabs, for example, were in existence when the dinosaurs ruled the earth. All are still in existence.

Deadly Disease

A fourth theory involving dinosaur weakness supposes that a particularly deadly disease developed and spread rapidly around the world. It destroyed the dinosaurs before they could adapt mechanisms to combat it. The dinosaurs were too slow in developing antibodies to survive the onslaught of such a disease.

This theory is based on the fact that naturally occurring epidemics do destroy large numbers of a single species. Hoof-and-mouth disease among cows, unless checked by medicine, spreads rapidly and over wide areas. Between A.D. 1348 and 1350 the bubonic plague, or Black Death, killed one-fifth to one-third of the human population of Europe, Asia, and Africa.

> *The activity of dinosaurs was more sedate than that of mammals. The basic strategy of dinosaurs in general was 'slow and steady,' and what it lacked in mammalian elan, it made up in economy."*
> Scientist Nicholas Hotton III,
> Smithsonian Institution

The prime argument against this theory lies in its peculiarly selective nature. Hoof-and-mouth disease kills cows. The bubonic plague kills people and animals but not plants. What sort of epidemic could kill 70 percent of the plant and animal life on earth, yet leave 30 percent untouched?

Species extinctions and replacements have occurred continually throughout earth's history. Some dinosaurs had become extinct even before the mass extinction of 65 million years ago. *Stegosaurus* died out long before the end of the Cretaceous era when *Tyrannosaurus* was in its prime. Extinction is a natural process. But what disease could destroy some 340 varieties of dinosaurs as well as half of the flowering plants? What type of disease could account for the simultaneous end of the soaring pterosaurs as well as the gigantic marine reptiles, the mosasaurs, and plesiosaurs?

> *The idea that Tyrannosaurus plodded along like some slow, dim-witted creature is simply not true. He was not a shuffler."*
> *Paleontologist Robert T. Bakker, University of Colorado Museum*

The disease theory is difficult to prove or disprove. A few bacteria fossils have been found. Yet there is no way to tell what their effect might have been upon other organisms. This is another of Dr. Gould's "perennial untestable speculations."

Some scientists have pointed to plants as the agents that caused the dinosaurs' deaths. Drastic changes in plants may

have led to dinosaur starvation or made many plants poisonous to dinosaurs. There is even one theory that dinosaurs may have overdosed after becoming addicted to deadly drugs contained in some plants.

Scientist Robert T. Bakker theorizes that the evolution of flowering plants was a direct result of dinosaur feeding habits. At the beginning of the Cretaceous period, grazing dinosaurs often stripped large areas of vegetation. The most successful plants in such an environment would have been those that could rapidly grow new leaves and spread to bare areas. Flowering plants have that capability and, in a manner of speaking, took advantage of the situation. Toward the end of the dinosaurs' reign, those flowering plants spread dramatically.

Death by Overdose

Scientist Anthony Swain suggested that the dinosaurs died from overdoses of amino acid-based alkaloids contained in many of these plants. Dr. Swain based his theory on the fact that some flowering plants produce bitter-tasting alkaloids that make up naturally occurring drugs like nicotine and morphine. The dinosaurs, he theorizes, became addicted to the drugs in plants and died of massive drug overdoses.

Dr. Swain argued that the plant-eating dinosaurs, some of which ate as much as a ton a day, did not evolve effective mechanisms to taste the bitterness of flowering plants. Nor did their livers evolve rapidly enough to detoxify the alkaloids present in those plants. The result, he claimed, was

Paleontologist Robert T. Bakker: "It all started very suddenly, in the spring of 1955. I was reading magazines in my grandfather's house in New Jersey, and I found that magical Life cover story—''Dinosaurs.'' . . . I discovered an entire world. . . . And I made up my mind then and there that I would devote my life to the dinosaurs."

death on a massive scale. He suggested that the distorted positions in which many dinosaur fossils have been found are due to the agonizing contortions brought on by death by overdose.

Dr. Stephen Jay Gould, however, emphatically disagrees, calling the theory "simply a gratuitous, attention-grabbing guess. It cannot be tested," he says, "for how can we know what dinosaurs tasted or what their livers could do?" Furthermore, according to Gould, the contortions of dinosaur fossils are a perfectly natural occurrence that do nothing to back up the theory of death by overdose. "Muscles contract after death and geological strata rise and fall with the motions of the earth's crust after burial—more than enough reason to distort a fossil's pristine appearance," Gould writes.

> **"** *If they ate mainly one plant, just as the koala bear lives on eucalyptus, they would be in trouble if that plant were no longer available."*
>
> James Hopson, University of Chicago

Others who disagree point out that flowering plants were in existence millions of years before the dinosaurs became extinct. If the plants were responsible for that extinction, why did it take them so long to accomplish it? Nor does the theory address the fact that thousands of plants became extinct along with the dinosaurs.

Starving Titans

Might the dinosaurs have died of starvation? Some scientists believe so. Herbivorous dinosaurs were accustomed to eating ferns and flowering plants, they maintain, but around this time grasses began to proliferate. Ferns and flowering plants decreased. These dinosaurs, unfortunately, were not equipped with the right kinds of teeth to chew the new grasses. They slowly died of starvation.

> *The dinosaurs of late Cretaceous times did live in modern forests . . . so if there was a change in food supply that affected the plant-eating dinosaurs, it was too subtle to be registered in the geologic record."*
> Paleontologist Edwin H. Colbert,
> American Museum of Natural History

Another plant-related theory proposes that the mass extinction of dinosaurs was caused by caterpillars that fed on the leaves of plants. Today, natural enemies like birds keep down the numbers of caterpillars, but when caterpillars first appeared, the few birds present apparently did not eat them. The caterpillars may have eaten so many plants that there were none left for the plant-eating dinosaurs. The plant-eating dinosaurs died out; their meat-eating cousins who preyed on them soon followed. Eventually no dinosaurs were left.

Opponents seriously question the validity of these theories. If plants somehow led to the death of the dinosaurs, they ask, why then did over 50 percent of these

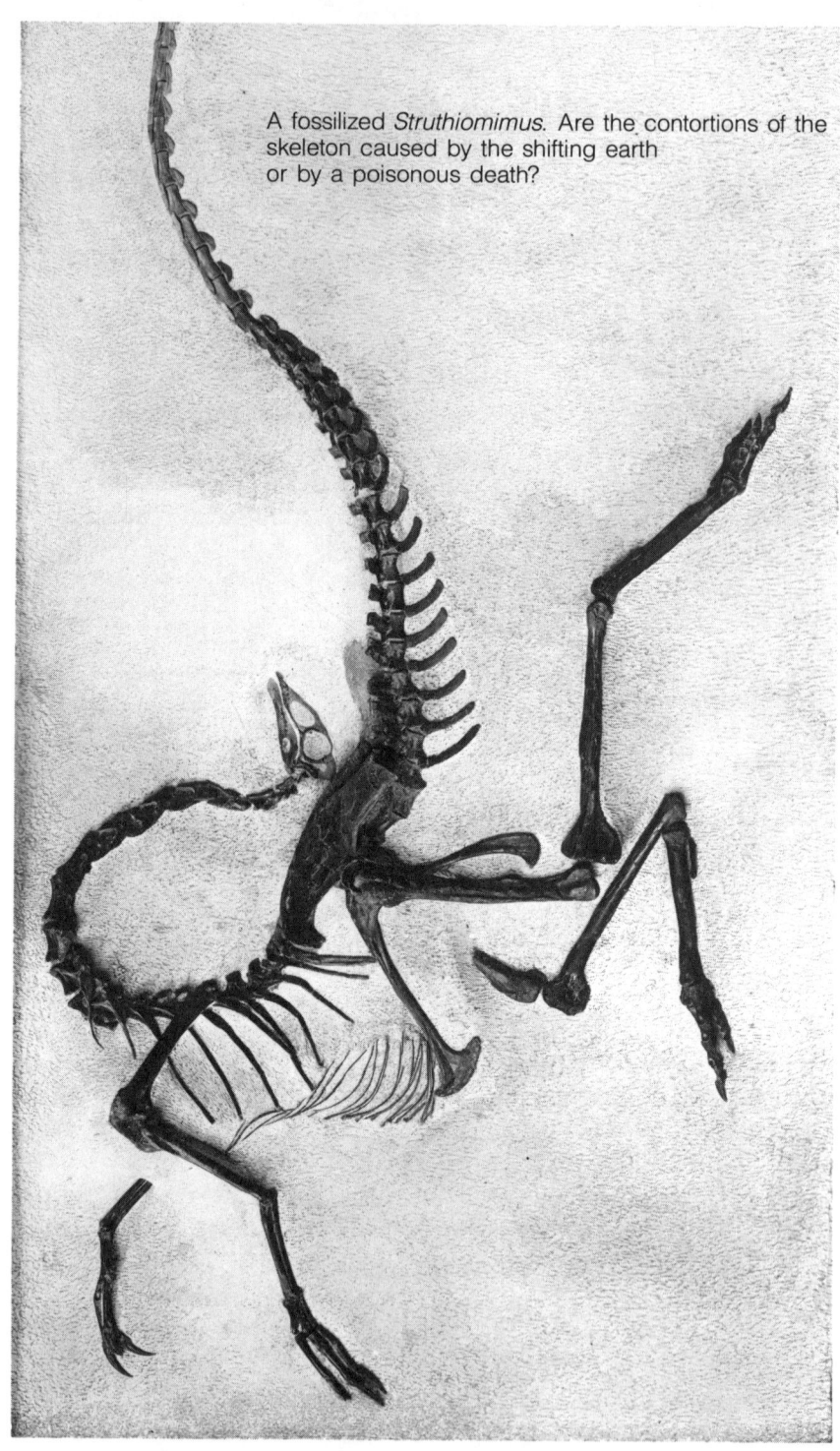

A fossilized *Struthiomimus*. Are the contortions of the skeleton caused by the shifting earth or by a poisonous death?

same plants also become extinct? Why did marine animals like ammonites die out along with all marine reptiles except turtles? What could account for the deaths of so many, varied species?

Three

Climate as Killer

A major change in climate at the end of the Cretaceous period has long been considered a likely cause of the death of the dinosaurs. The climate of the Cretaceous period, as shown by fossil evidence of plant life, was tropical throughout much of the world. One-half of the plants then living were tropical ferns and cycads, which were lush, palmlike plants. Both needed constant heat to survive. Heat-loving plankton flourished in the warm, shallow Cretaceous seas. And dinosaurs dominated the landscape. Then, according to one major climatic theory, the earth's climate suddenly began to cool, setting up conditions that led to the demise of the dinosaurs.

There is evidence that such a cooling-off did occur at this time. Fossil plankton show a dramatic decrease in size and quantity. A logical scientific deduction is that the oceans and seas had become too cold for them to survive. Fossilized

plant pollen provides evidence that only one-third of the plants during the Tertiary period were tropical as opposed to one-half during the earlier period. Fossils from the Tertiary period show an increased number of plants like evergreens, which are able to withstand colder temperatures. And fossils of cycads, one of the primary foods of plant-eating dinosaurs, suddenly disappear, yet another indication of rapid cooling.

The theory that a severe climatic cooling laid waste to the dinosaurs has many supporters. One of their key arguments is that dinosaurs, unequipped with feathers or fur for insulation, would have been unable to survive any deep or prolonged drop in temperature. If the cold weather alone didn't kill them, the death of the cycads would have removed one of their principal sources of food. Without plants to eat, the herbivores would have perished, eliminating the food supply of the carnivores that preyed on them. Supporters of this theory also point out that if the temperature drop killed the plankton, the key to the oceanic food chain, then the large marine reptiles, deprived of their main food source, would have died as well.

> *I just can't see any way to maintain there wasn't a mass extinction. You look at the reefs in the Caribbean, at the fossils from the Cretaceous, and you look three inches up and you can tell the world has changed."*
> *Professor David Jablonski, University of Chicago*

This theory, many scientists claim, does explain why some mammals, birds, reptiles, and plants were able to survive when the dinosaurs and other plants and animals were not. Mammals and birds covered with fur and feathers would have been able to withstand the cold. Small reptiles could have burrowed into holes in the dirt or mud. Plant seeds could have lain dormant for tens, hundreds, maybe thousands of years. (Tomatoes have been grown from 2,000-year-old seeds.)

Opponents to the theory dispute that a sudden drop in temperature ever occurred. Edwin Colbert, a leading

> "*Catastrophe theories are very seductive. They seem to explain complex events very simply. . . . My own analysis of the fossil record suggests that Cretaceous extinctions were gradual and that the catastrophe theory is wrong.*"
>
> Professor Robert Sloan, University of Minnesota

dinosaur expert, writes in his book *Dinosaurs, An Illustrated History*, that "The changes did not take place suddenly. From the fossil evidence it is difficult to see much climatic difference between late Cretaceous and early Cenozoic time. . . . No drastic change can be detected that would have brought about the end of all of the dinosaurs."

Colbert also questions the survival of reptiles like snakes and crocodiles if the cold killed the dinosaurs. These cold-blooded creatures also cannot tolerate extreme or prolonged cold weather. "If the crocodiles could make it, why not some of the dinosaurs?" Colbert asks.

A variation on the cooling theory is the theory of alternating seasons. Whereas at one time the climate on earth was that of perpetual summer, around the middle of the late Cretaceous period seasons began to develop. Some scientists argue that the summers became extremely hot and the winters harsh and bitter. This drastic changing of climate was enough to cause the extinctions. Other scientists disagree, pointing out that seasons developed some 15-20

Paleontologist Edwin H. Colbert: "*We display the extent of our ignorance upon a subject that is at once baffling and intriguing, a subject that is hard to pass by without a few theories. Such will be the problem of dinosaurian extinction for years to come; many people will speculate on it, but no one will have any definite answers, at least not until much more is known.*"

The Greenhouse Effect: Heat from the sun is "trapped" by the Earth's atmosphere in much the same way that the glass panes of a greenhouse trap the heat. More carbon dioxide in the atmosphere makes the "greenhouse panes" more effective, trapping more heat and causing the Earth's temperature to rise. Some of the things that increase carbon dioxide

million years before the dinosaurs died. Dinosaurs had adapted to climatic changes in the past. Given 15 million years, they certainly would have adapted to this new change.

The Greenhouse Effect

Another climatic theory, one opposite the cooling argument, proposes that the dinosaurs died due to an increase in heat. This theory suggests that the earth warmed dramatically at the end of the Cretaceous period. The warming was triggered by the retreat of shallow inland seas like the one that once stretched from the Gulf of Mexico as far north as present-day Missouri. As the seas receded, the marine plants and algae, prime consumers of carbon dioxide, died in vast quantities. The carbon dioxide not consumed by these plants built up in the atmosphere and trapped the heat, dramatically raising temperatures around the globe. This is called the "greenhouse effect." Dinosaurs, unable to protect

are volcanos, clouds, water vapor, air pollution, and the loss of great numbers of plants. A drastic increase in carbon dioxide would cause a drastic temperature rise in the Earth's climate and the deaths of any plants or animals which could not adapt to such a dramatic change.

themselves against the heat, perished.

Fossilized dinosaur eggshells also suggest a climatic warming. The shells became thinner and more fragile around this time, typical of eggs in warm climates. Some modern birds respond similarly when temperatures rise, laying eggs with thinner shells than normal. Large numbers of these thin dinosaur eggshells have been discovered from the late Cretaceous period.

Many unhatched eggs from this period have also been found. Some scientists think that these unhatched eggs were never fertilized. They say that even a small rise or drop in the temperature could have affected the testes of male dinosaurs, making them unable to produce sperm. The dinosaurs, unable to fertilize their eggs, died out.

The main argument against the sterilization theory is that it is untestable. The fossil record does not provide physical evidence to indicate exact dinosaur body temperature, much less the temperature at which their reproductive systems would not function. Dr. Stephen Jay Gould writes, "Testicles

Mount St. Helens in the state of Washington, erupting on May 18, 1980.

simply don't fossilize and how could we infer their temperature tolerances if they did?" He concludes that this theory "is simply untestable and unusable."

A fourth climate-related explanation for the death of the dinosaurs involves an increase or decrease in rainfall. A decrease would have caused swamps and lakes to dry. Dinosaurs apparently thrived in humid environments; their disappearance would have caused great stress on the animals.

Conversely, an increase in rainfall would have meant flooding of the dinosaurs' habitats. In either case, the environment of the dinosaurs would have been destroyed, and that destruction could possibly have ended their existence.

Shifting the Blame

Most fossil evidence indicates that there *was* a severe climatic change at the end of the Cretaceous period, and that plants and animals that had thrived in the previously stable climate were unable to deal successfully with this change. Whether the change was geologically rapid, occurring over a million or even a thousand years, or dramatically faster,

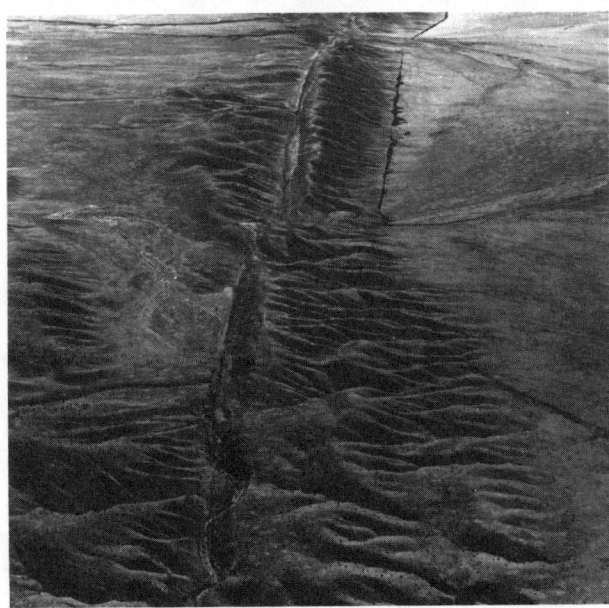

California's San Andreas Fault.

> *"The climate was changing at the end of the Mezozoic Era and the beginnings of change can be detected in the Cretaceous. . . . But that, of course, was not why the dinosaurs disappeared. They disappeared because a catastrophic event took place."*
> *Author Michael Allaby and physicist James Lovelock*, The Great Extinction

happening in a decade or a matter of days, the question remains: What could have caused such a change?

Many geologists think the earth itself triggered radical climatic changes. They believe that shifting of continents, tremendous volcanic eruptions, and the uplifting of mountain ranges, either singly or in combination, could have altered the climate enough to end the days of the dinosaurs.

The earliest dinosaurs lived when the only visible land on earth was Pangaea, one gigantic supercontinent. Pangaea began to break up 190 million years ago. The smaller land masses created from this break-up have been shifting ever since. In fact, the continents are still drifting today. Some, like North America and Europe, are moving farther apart. Others, like Europe and Africa, are slowly coming together.

The movements of drifting continents, exploding volcanoes, and shifting mountains have put tremendous

strains on the earth's crust, causing extensive faulting and earthquakes. California's San Andreas Fault is a modern example. Volcanoes, such as Mount St. Helens and others that dot the northwestern United States, are modern-day indicators of the forces at work deep within the earth.

During the early Mesozoic era when Pangaea was in the process of breaking up, volcanic eruptions and earthquakes were much more common than they are today. Tons of volcanic ash blasting into the skies could have dramatically altered weather patterns. When Mount Tambora in Indonesia erupted in 1815, billions of tons of pulverized rock and ash rose into the sky, creating clouds so thick they blocked the sunshine. A year later, the effects of that ash cloud were felt as far away as New England. During "The Year Without a Summer," New Englanders suffered six inches of snow in June and frost in July and August. Temperatures dropped worldwide. If enough volcanoes of this size were to erupt at the same time, the volume of volcanic ash in the atmosphere would effectively filter out so much sunlight that the entire planet would cool. Plants and animals would suffer tremendously and possibly even die out.

> *There is not much question that something did happen. The debate is about what the results were. Most of us will admit that in all probability the impact had some influence. It's just that we don't all agree it was catastrophic. . . . There was a great impact, but it hit in the midst of a situation that was already fraught with change."*
>   Professor Keith Rigby Jr., University of
>   Notre Dame

Erupting volcanoes might also have caused an increase of carbon dioxide in the atmosphere, creating the "greenhouse effect" discussed earlier. By trapping the sun's energy inside the atmosphere, the carbon dioxide could have caused the temperatures of water, land, and air to rise.

Another geologic event that could have triggered dramatic climatic changes might have been the unleashing of a vast

amount of water from the Arctic. This theory is based on the premise that a freshwater ocean existed in the Arctic before the continents broke apart. According to this theory, when Norway and Greenland separated, the freshwater ocean flooded into the other salty oceans. So much fresh water would have reduced the salinity of the other oceans and lowered their temperatures by some twenty degrees centigrade. Because cooler water evaporates more slowly than warm water, and rainfall is dependent on water vapor in the air, a decrease of rain would have occurred, causing droughts. The result would have been death on a massive scale for plants and animals.

The drawback to this theory is that there is no conclusive proof that the Arctic Ocean was once a freshwater sea. But there are some scientists who don't believe that the salinity of the water would have made much difference. If freezing waters around the poles had invaded tropical waters, they say, this, too, would have led to a drop in worldwide water temperatures, and the results would have been similar.

> " *A chance meteorite may have polished off the dinosaurs. But until its place of impact is discovered, it's just as well not to rule out terrestrial suspects—like change of climate."*
> Paleontologist Antoni Hoffman,
> Columbia University

Two major objections have been raised to counter theories that volcanic eruptions and/or the shifting of land masses created climatic changes severe enough to wipe out the dinosaurs. The first is best stated by Dale Russell of the National Museum of Ottawa, Canada. "Organisms are too wonderfully plastic," he says. "It is hard to accept that more of them would not have found ways to adapt to gradual changes in the environment." Many other scientists agree with Russell since these geologic theories all assume prolonged time to bring about climatic changes.

The second major argument opposing these theories concerns the selective nature of the extinctions. Why did

> "*I simply do not understand why some paleontologists—who are really the people that told us all about the extinctions... —now seem to deny that there ever was a catastrophic extinction.*"
> Scientist Walter Alvarez, University of California, Berkeley

some species survive the climatic changes while others did not?

Maybe, some scientists believe, the changes in climate were not gradual at all but catastrophically sudden. What could have triggered devastating changes overnight? To search for an answer, these scientists looked to the sky.

Four

Cosmic Collision

Could an asteroid colliding with the earth have caused the extinction of the dinosaurs? This theory, first proposed in 1979 by Nobel-Prize-winning physicist Luis Alvarez, has intrigued numerous scientists. Alvarez, examining a thin (1 cm) layer of clay from the end of the Cretaceous period, discovered the clay contained thirty times the normal amount of the element iridium. Although rare on earth, iridium is plentiful in cosmic material like meteors, asteroids, and comets. Alvarez, trying to account for the high proportion of iridium in his clay sample, proposed that around 65 million years ago, an asteroid collided with the earth. He concluded that the impact of such a collision might well have led to the mass extinction of the dinosaurs.

Alvarez suggested that the earth-shattering asteroid was some six miles across and traveled at a speed of 40,000 miles per hour. It smashed into the earth creating a crater 100

miles in diameter. It hurled up a cloud of pulverized rock that quickly spread around the globe, cutting off sunlight for several years. Day turned into night. The sunlight able to filter through the dust would have been equal to only 10 percent of the light from a full moon. With the sunlight blocked, temperatures would have dropped dramatically. Photosynthesis would have stopped, and plants would have begun to die. The plant-eating dinosaurs would have starved, and the meat-eaters would soon have followed. All this could have happened with amazing speed. An asteroid cloud could have covered the earth within weeks. The dinosaurs would have been extinct within a few years.

> *Three years of intensive investigations by a variety of scientific groups have left the nuclear winter hypothesis essentially intact."*
> Curt Covey, Rosenstiel School of Marine and Atmospheric Science, University of Miami

As soon as Luis Alvarez and his son Walter, a geologist, announced this theory, scientists around the world began to ask questions. Was such a collision really possible? Where did the asteroid hit the earth? Why weren't *all* of the plants and animals killed?

The Alvarez team tackled the questions as they arose.

Do such catastrophic cosmic collisions actually occur? A glance at the Moon on a clear night provides an immediate

Scientists Walter and Luis Alvarez. Walter: "Perhaps we will never understand the killing process in detail; we have no way to know whether the . . . fossil dinosaur [highest in the Earth's layers] was even alive at the time of the impact, let alone ask him exactly what it was that did him in."

answer. Pockmarked by numerous impact craters, the Moon preserves evidence of past collisions. Mercury's surface, too, is covered with craters. So are some of the moons of Jupiter and Saturn. Similar impacts have occurred on Earth. Meteor Crater in Arizona is a prime example of an impact crater. It is theorized that some 200 impact craters exist around the world.

> *If you're going to have a nuclear winter killing off the dinosaurs, why didn't it kill off everything else?"*
>
> *Paleontologist Walter Clemens, University of California Berkeley*

Then why don't we see more of them? "The reason," says Dr. Eugene Shoemaker, a leading planetary geologist, "is that the earth is so active. The movements of the Earth's plates, the creation of mountain ranges, the effect of erosion by wind and water, tend to remove all traces of craters." Meteor Crater, 600 feet deep and 4,000 feet across, is already suffering from heavy erosion, and it is less than 25,000 years old. An asteroid crater 65 million years old would certainly have suffered much heavier erosion.

Where Is the Evidence?

Opposing scientists argue that an asteroid large enough to cause the extinction of the dinosaurs must have left traces of a crater somewhere. Not necessarily, counters Luis Alvarez—especially if the asteroid landed in the ocean. Such an impact in the ocean would have instantly vaporized much of the asteroid as well as a massive amount of water. The remaining piece of the asteroid would have created a crater on the ocean floor. And the ocean floor is so geologically active that in 65 million years all traces of the crater would have disappeared.

The search for an asteroid-impact crater continues, however. John McHone and Robert Dietz of Arizona State University at Tempe have been studying impact craters all over the world. Although they have found some craters that are the right age, most have been too small to have caused the global effects Alvarez describes. One, however, the Kara crater in the Soviet Union, might provide the answer. This crater is dated at about 60 million years old and consists of two indentations, one 37 miles wide, the other 16 miles wide. The doublet or cluster of asteroids that caused the Kara crater would have released more energy than a single, larger asteroid. Continuing research may yet prove Kara to be the asteroid-impact crater that Luis Alvarez theorizes brought about the end of the dinosaurs.

Mysteriously Selective Extinctions

Evidence has recently been found in Montana, however, that seriously weakens the asteroid extinction theory. At Hell Creek, a geologic formation showing the transition from dinosaurs to mammals is well *below* the iridium layer. This indicates that the dinosaurs died out long before the iridium layer was deposited.

Another serious argument against the asteroid theory comes from the selective nature of the extinction. While all of the dinosaurs and 50-70 percent of other plant and animal life perished at the end of the Cretaceous period, not all life

The pocked surface of the Moon.

died out. Why did some of the birds, turtles, sharks, crocodiles, small land mammals, and lizards survive? If sunlight was blocked by the asteroid-impact cloud, then why didn't all photosynthesizing plants die?

Dr. Alvarez answers that the animals that survived fed upon the nuts, seeds, decaying vegetation, and insects still around after the asteroid impact. He theorizes that all plants did die, but that seed-bearing plants (whose seeds could have lain dormant during the five to ten years before the asteroid cloud settled) returned when their seeds were able to germinate again. Spores and hardy roots of other plants could have lived through the impact to grow new plants later.

Regular Mass Extinctions

Dr. Edwin Colert, Curator of Vertebrate Paleontology at the Museum of Northern Arizona, counters that the extinction of plants that did occur did not happen at the same time as the extinction of the dinosaurs. Dr. Leo Hickey of the Smithsonian Institute agrees. "Looking at the plant evidence across the Cretaceous-Tertiary boundary here [in northern Wyoming]," he states, "we see no evidence of an asteroid impact." He adds, "I'd love for it to have been a

Meteor Crater in Arizona.

catastrophe because it makes things simpler. But my work doesn't show it."

New evidence from chemists at the University of Maryland challenges Alvarez's theory that the high iridium levels come from an extraterrestrial source. They have reported that recent eruptions of the Kilauea volcano in Hawaii have contained unexpectedly high levels of iridium. This suggests that volcanic eruptions may have caused the high iridium contents of the rocks Alvarez studied.

> *Most researchers agree that a comet could have done the deed, by striking the Earth and clouding the atmosphere with debris, plunging the planet into an epoch of cold weather to which many of the most exquisitely evolved creatures could not adapt in time to survive. The killer need not have been very large: a chunk of stone only 10 miles in diameter, hitting the Earth at a velocity of, say, 100,000 miles per hour, would explode with a force equal to 10,000 times that of all the deliverable nuclear warheads in the world."*
>
> Author Timothy Ferris, Science Digest, *July 1984*

The asteroid theory raises many more questions than it answers. One of those questions involves the nature of mass extinctions on earth. Geologists know that mass extinctions have occurred on earth many times during the past 600 million years. For example, 248 million years ago, between the Permian and the Triassic periods, it is estimated that over 90 percent of all species died. Were mass extinctions such as this one simply random events, or were they predictable?

Geologists have recently determined that such extinctions may indeed occur in periodic cycles. Geologists David Raup and Jack Sepkoski statistically analyzed fossil families. They found that over the past 225 million years, a mass extinction

> **"** *No one has yet discovered the huge 65 million-year-old crater that such a collision would have left."*
>
> Writer Joseph Wisnowsky, Time, February 17, 1986

of life on land occurred every 26 million years. An earlier calculation by two Princeton geologists determined that mass extinctions of sea life occurred every 32 million years. What could account for such regular extinction cycles?

The Nemesis Theory

Richard Muller, a former student of Luis Alvarez and now his colleague, was searching for a model that would explain a periodic bombardment of earth by asteroids. Muller came up with the idea that our sun might be a binary, or twin, star. Twin stars are a pair of stars that revolve about a common point. "Two-thirds of all known stars belong to multiple star systems," says Muller, "so it is not unusual that the sun might have a companion." Muller named his sun twin Nemesis after the Greek goddess who punished the proud and powerful. Can it be that the gravitational force of Nemesis periodically draws asteroids toward earth, thereby causing mass extinctions every 26-30

Comet Bennett.

Astrophysicist Daniel P. Whitmire: *"Just the possibility that life here has been controlled by an astronomical event is very far-reaching."*

million years?

Muller thought that if our sun had a twin, and if that twin's orbit passed by the asteroid belt found between Mars and Jupiter, then this sun twin could propel asteroids toward Earth on a regular basis. Unfortunately, Muller could not find data to support his idea.

Comet Showers

Another scientist, Piet Hut, suggested to Muller that the theory might work if Nemesis disturbed comets rather than asteroids. Comets are composed of frozen gases and dust. They are every bit as lethal in collision as asteroids. Scientists believe that there is an immense halo of billions of comets orbiting our solar system. This collection of comets has been named the "Oort Cloud" after the Dutch astronomer Jan Oort who proposed its existence. Although this cloud of comets has never been seen, most scientists believe it exists. If Nemesis were to sweep by the Oort cloud during its orbit, its gravitational pull would dislodge a billion comets. These comets would travel toward the inner regions of our solar system for some 1-3 million years. At least one of these comets, probably many more, would eventually collide with Earth.

Richard Muller theorizes that his twin sun orbits near the Oort cloud only once every 26-30 million years. The comet shower it would create would therefore coincide with mass extinctions on Earth.

Luis Alvarez tried to poke holes in Muller's theory, but Muller was able to successfully defend it. Moreover, Alvarez found that a comet would fit into his own theory as well as an asteroid. The results of either would have been essentially

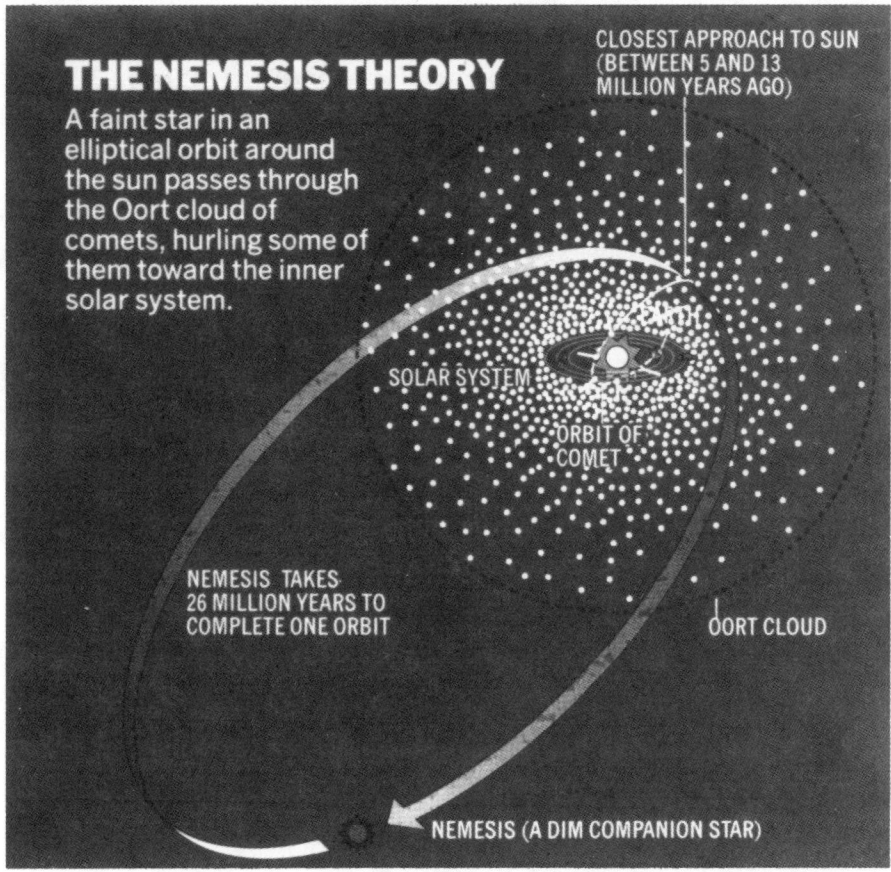

the same.

Walter Alvarez then suggested that there should be evidence of impacts in the rock record if comets or asteroids periodically showered the earth. Both would produce similar impact craters. He and Muller studied data on thirteen large craters and found that the craters fit into a 28.4-million-year cycle. This data supported Muller's Nemesis theory of periodic bombardment every 26-30 million years.

Other researchers have found more evidence in support of Muller's theory in a Cretaceous-Tertiary boundary rock layer in Montana. Not only is iridium present in the claystone, but the shape of the clay particles and the structure and type of quartz present is characteristic of impact craters. This suggests that impact craters coincide

> *Many geologists, including myself, have long found themselves in the uncomfortable position of viewing extraterrestrial catastrophes as inherently plausible but rooting against them because we knew no way of obtaining evidence for such catasphrophes even if they had occurred. The asteroidal theory has changed all that."*
>
> Geologist Stephen Jay Gould, Harvard University

Skeleton of a *Tyrannosaurus*: Mighty giant felled by a comet?

with the extinction of the dinosaurs.

There are certainly some problems with the Nemesis theory. One of them is that Nemesis' elliptical orbit is believed to be more than two light years across. (Light travels at the speed of about 186,000 miles per second. The

> "*Many consider all the newfangled extraterrestrial scenarios to be half-baked takeoffs of H.G. Wells. . . . It's science gone absolutely bonkers.*"
> Paleontologist Dewey McLean, Virginia Polytechnic Institute

distance of a light year would be about 6 trillion miles.) Being so far apart would reduce the gravitational attraction between the two stars, and Nemesis, if it exists at all, may well have been bumped out of orbit by another star. "Nemesis may have serious problems of stability," says astronomer Daniel Whitmire. "Over the age of the solar system, the period of its orbit would change drastically." An unstable orbit would, of course, reduce the chances that Nemesis is to blame for regular mass extinctions on Earth.

Astrogeologist Eugene Shoemaker argues that the extinction cycle may be only a matter of coincidence. "I give [Muller's] idea less than a 1 percent chance of being correct," he says.

Another major problem of the Nemesis theory is that no companion star has been located. Does it really exist? Muller and other scientists are still scanning the cosmos, hoping to discover their elusive Nemesis.

Five

More Heavenly Theories

When we study dinosaurs, we look deep into the earth to find their fossils. When we study dinosaur extinction, we are more and more frequently looking to the heavens.

Planet X

Astronomer Daniel Whitmire believes with Muller and Hut that a shower of comets may have led to the dinosaurs' demise. He theorizes, however, that the cause of that rain of comets is not Nemesis but a tenth, as yet undiscovered, planet in our solar system. He calls it Planet X.

Since the late 1800s, scientists have predicted the existence of other planets in our solar system. As late as 1930, Pluto was discovered. But Pluto did not completely account for the irregularity in the planetary orbit of Uranus. A tenth planet might help to explain the discrepancies in the

Physicist Richard Muller: *"To be an explorer today is to be a scientist."*

movements of the outer planets, Uranus and Neptune.

Whitmire and his colleague John Matese calculate that Planet X revolves around our sun once every 1,000 years. Its orbit is thought to be highly elongated. Due to the gravitational pull of the other planets, the orbit also shifts. This shifting could account for the irregularities in the orbit of Uranus. Planet X's peculiar path could also bring it close to the Oort cloud only once every 28 million years—close enough to dislodge comets and propel them toward earth.

As is true with the Nemesis star, no one has observed this tenth planet. Whitmire himself admits that verification of it must "come in the observing." Nevertheless, its existence would account for other phenomena in our solar system.

Richard Muller feels that, "If I had come up with [the Planet X theory], I would have thrown it out because I doubt very much that a planet could cause that particular kind of comet shower." Whitmire counters that the orbit of Planet X brings it much closer to the Sun than that of Nemesis, and that *increases* the likelihood of comets striking the Earth.

Cosmic Dust

Michael Rampino and Richard Stothers of Goddard Institute for Space Studies suggest another possible reason for a cycle of comet bombardment—cosmic dust.

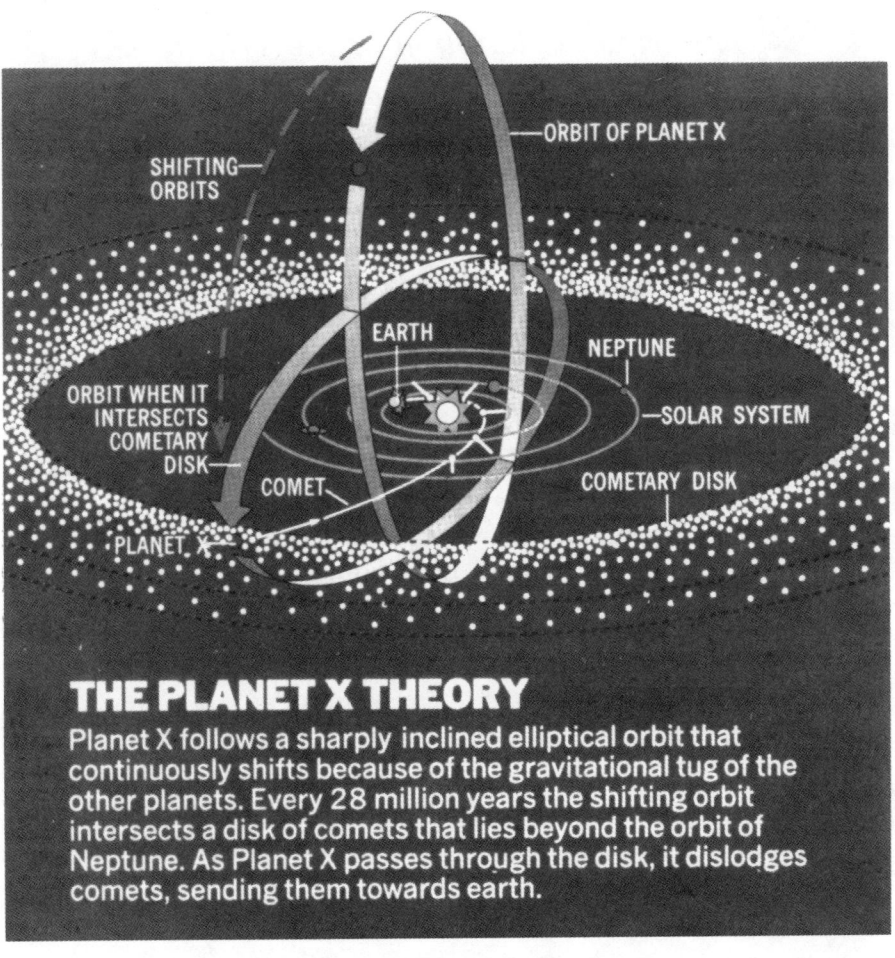

THE PLANET X THEORY
Planet X follows a sharply inclined elliptical orbit that continuously shifts because of the gravitational tug of the other planets. Every 28 million years the shifting orbit intersects a disk of comets that lies beyond the orbit of Neptune. As Planet X passes through the disk, it dislodges comets, sending them towards earth.

As our solar system moves through the Milky Way galaxy, it passes through regions where stars and dust clouds are more concentrated. Rampino and Stothers believe that it may be these dust clouds that jar comets loose from the Oort cloud. They propose that our solar system encounters the dustiest portion of the galaxy every 33 million years—a figure that almost fits with mass extinction cycles on earth.

Some opponents argue that no one is sure just how clouds of galactic material are distributed throughout the galaxy. Others have pointed out that our sun is currently close to one of these dusty regions. But the last major extinction occurred 11 million years ago, and there is no

> *The triple assumption of the Whitmire-Matese model—a hitherto undetected planet; a new belt of cometary orbits, smaller than the Oort cloud; and an elongated, precessing orbit for Planet X—has proved too far-fetched for most astronomers to accept."*
> Astronomer Donald Goldsmith, Nemesis: The Death-Star and Other Theories of Mass Extinction

evidence that another is about to happen now.

Physicist Patrick Thaddeus explains that these dust clouds are widely distributed throughout the galaxy. The comet belt, or Oort cloud, should encounter dust-filled regions frequently. He suggests that his Goddard colleagues' calculations are "just the wrong numbers."

Supernova

In the 1950s, Russian scientist Iosef Shlovsky suggested that a supernova explosion might have caused the extinction of the dinosaurs.

Stars are believed to go through a life cycle. They are born when gravity pulls together gas and dust, and the internal temperature increases enough to produce a nuclear

Allosaurus fragilis: Victim of a catastrophe or of the natural changes in the world?

reaction. As the nuclear reaction continues, the star's temperature builds. The star gets heavier and bigger. Giant stars then cool and shrink as hydrogen is used in the nuclear reaction. However, sometimes an exceptionally large star can explode; it is so massive that it can no longer hold itself together. This explosion is called a supernova. Supernovas release tremendous amounts of energy in the form of light, heat, x-rays, and gamma rays. Could radiation from the explosion of one of these superstars have bombarded the earth, causing the extinction of the dinosaurs?

About three supernovas are observed each century. These explosions, however, have occurred trillions of miles away from the earth. Chinese records from the year 1054 describe the explosion of a supernova about 5,000 light years, or approximately 30,000 trillion miles, away. The light was so intense that it was visible to the naked eye during the day.

> *"Whatever the details, [the evidence] very strongly implicates an extraterrestrial mechanism."*
>
> Paleontologist John J. Sepkoski Jr., University of Chicago

Scientists believe that if a star exploded within a few hundred light years of earth, the energy released would have a disastrous affect on life here. The cosmic radiation bombarding earth would cause most life to be killed outright. Much of the surviving life would suffer from cancer, sterility, or abnormal offspring.

A blast like this could explain why the dinosaurs and most other life forms became extinct 65 million years ago. But how could *any* life survive such a blast? We know that 30 percent of the animals and plants on earth *did* survive the mass extinction.

The mammals of the Cretaceous period were small. According to proponents of the supernova theory, they burrowed underground and thereby reduced their exposure to the cosmic radiation. Even crocodiles could have buried themselves in mud, which would have increased their chances of survival. However, large animals, like most of the

Soot layer at Hell's Creek, Montana. The dark stripe running through the hill is part of the evidence that suggests that wildfires may have destroyed the dinosaurs.

dinosaurs, would have had nowhere to hide, and they would have died.

But why did much of the life in the oceans, both large marine animals like the plesiosaurs and icthyosaurs and small marine organisms like the foraminifera become extinct along with the dinosaurs? The water could have shielded these organisms from the full effects of a supernova's radiation just as effectively as dirt or mud shielded mammals and crocodiles.

The answer could possibly be that a supernova explosion was responsible for a sudden and extreme drop in temperature. As we have seen, this, too, could have caused the dinosaurs to die out.

Luis and Walter Alvarez did consider a supernova explosion when their research led them to contemplate an extraterrestrial cause for the mass extinctions at the end of the Cretaceous period. A supernova explosion would explain the iridium they found in the clay and rocks they studied. However, they determined that these deposits of iridium were not what scientists would expect to find from the explosion of a supernova. There should also have been desposits of other rare elements like Plutonium-244, but there were none. Scientists from the Geological Institute of Amsterdam as well as other laboratories analyzed rock samples for the chemical "fingerprints" that a supernova

explosion would have left. None were found.

The discovery of a worldwide layer of soot has sparked a new extinction theory. Three researchers from the University of Chicago argue that the "surprisingly large amount of soot" came from a fire that swept the world 65 million years ago. They suggest that this fire was ignited by the impact of a huge comet or asteroid. These scientists say that the flames consumed oxygen and poisoned the atmosphere with carbon monoxide. It was smoke more than the dust of the impact cloud, they theorize, that cut off sunlight to the earth, causing temperatures to plummet and the dinosaurs to perish.

When they made their discovery, the team of scientists was examining clay samples from the same sediments that Luis Alvarez and his colleagues had examined. The samples, from Spain, Denmark, and New Zealand, contained substantial amounts of carbon soot like that deposited when vegetation burns.

"Wildfires," the scientists concluded, "seem to be the most plausible source of the soot layer."

These scientists linked their discovery with that of Luis Alvarez's impact theory to create another catastrophic version of the death of the dinosaurs. Their theory reinforces the impact theory.

> " *The last extinctions were not a single weekend of colossal slaughter but a drawn-out process requiring thousands and even millions of years."*
>
> Paleontologist Robert T. Bakker, University of Colorado Museum

Critics of this new theory question whether the soot could absorb enough sunlight to disrupt the climate on a worldwide scale. Their arguments are similar to those opposing the impact dust cloud theory. Could enough sunlight be blocked by such a cloud to stop photosynthesis around the globe? Why did some animals survive while the majority perished? Might the carbon in the samples have come from a comet or asteroid?

> "When the evidence strongly supports a more sudden, violent event, we will go where the evidence leads us. We may not like natural violence, but we cannot ignore it. Modern astronomy teaches us that the universe is a violent place."
>
> Geologist Walter Alvarez, University of California, Berkeley

Like the work of Alvarez and others, this theory raises new questions regarding the mass extinction at the end of the Cretaceous period. The search to disprove these new theories might well lead to the final explanation of the death of the dinosaurs.

Scientists agree that a solution to the dinosaurs' extinction will depend on more accurate dating of geological and fossil records. Astronomers need to provide more data to support the link between earth extinctions and events in outer space. From craters to comets, from fossils to star dust, scientists continue to probe our earth and our universe in their search for possible answers.

The Search Goes On

Dinosaurs in all their many shapes and sizes have fascinated scientists and lay people alike since their earliest discovery over 150 years ago. The mass extinction of these creatures, however, remains a tantalizing mystery. Even as we search the earth for clues or scan the skies for death stars, comets, and asteroids, no one single cause seems to answer all the questions raised by the death of the dinosaurs.

As Carl Sagan, author and scientist, wrote, "None of the explanations is anything like fully satisfying."

Yet as long as the mystery remains, we will continue to search for the answer, for who knows if a similar fate awaits us.

Books for Further Exploration

Jane Burton, *Time Exposure: A Photographic Record of the Dinosaur Age*. Beaufort Books, New York, 1984.

Daniel Cohen, *Monster Dinosaur*. Lippincott, New York, 1983.

Edwin H. Colbert, *Dinosaurs: An Illustrated History*. Hammond, New York, 1983.

Diagram Group, *A Field Guide to Dinosaurs*. Avon, New York, 1983.

Donald Glut, *The New Dinosaur Dictionary*. Citadel Press, Secaucus, NJ, 1984.

William Jaber, *Whatever Happened to the Dinosaurs?* Messner, New York, 1978.

David Lambert, *Dinosaur World*. Watts, New York, 1982.

Christopher Lampton, *Dinosaurs and the Age of Reptiles*. Watts, New York, 1983.

Christopher Lampton, *Mass Extinctions: One Theory of Why the Dinosaurs Vanished*. Watts, New York, 1986.

John C. McLoughlin, *Archosauria: A New Look at the Old Dinosaur*. Viking, New York, 1979.

Laurence Pringle, *Dinosaurs and People: Fossils, Facts, and Fantasies*. Harcourt Brace, New York, 1978.

Laurence Pringle, *Dinosaurs and Their World*. Harcourt Brace, New York, 1968.

Helen Sattler, *The Illustrated Dinosaur Dictionary*. Lothrop, New York, 1983.

William Elgin Swinton, *The Wonderful World of Prehistoric Animals*. Doubleday, Garden City, NY, 1969.

Glossary

General Terms

alkaloid bitter tasting substance that is the opposite of an acid
amber fossilized tree resin
ammonite extinct animal with a coiled, chambered shell
asteroid planetary rock material orbiting around the sun between Mars and Jupiter, ranging in size from 1 km. to over 700 km.
binary star two stars which revolve around a central point
carnivore meat-eating animal
comet mass of cosmic dust and ice that orbits the sun
decomposition the process of decaying
detoxify to get rid of the effect of a poison
dinosaurs extinct reptiles from the Mesozoic era including two distinct orders: *Ornithischia*, "bird-hipped," and *Saurischia*, "lizard-hipped"
earth's plates moving parts of the earth's crust
erode to wear away and transport earth's materials by agents such as wind, water, or ice
extinction the end of a species
fossil any impression, remains, or trace of a plant or animal from a past geological age
galaxy large group of stars
geologist scientist who studies the earth and its processes
greenhouse effect reflection of heat back to earth by carbon dioxide and water vapor in the atmosphere
herbivore plant-eating animal
iridium a rare metallic element
meteorite a piece of cosmic material which strikes the surface of a planet
mid-Atlantic ridge the mountain chain in the Atlantic Ocean which parallels the continental ridges
nuclear reaction changes within the center of an atom which produce energy
paleontologist scientist who studies ancient life
paleontology the scientific study of fossilized remains of animals and plants
photosynthesis the process plants use to produce food through the reaction of sunlight with the chlorophyll in the plant leaves
plankton tiny, passively floating or drifting animals and plants in a body of water

savannah grassland with scattered trees
scavenger an animal that eats dead or decaying organisms
sediment broken-down rocks and organic material deposited by water, ice, or wind
strata layer of rock
supernova an explosion of a star near the end of its life
theory a proposed explanation backed up by facts
uplift upheaval of the earth's crust over a long period of time

Geologic Time Terms
(see the chart on pp. 20-21)

Cenozoic geologic era following the Mesozoic and up to today; the first fossil evidence of modern humans is found in strata from late in this era
Cretaceous geologic time extending from 135 to 65 million years ago
Jurassic period of geologic time extending from 180 to 135 million years ago
Mesozoic geologic era of about 150 million years between the Paleozoic and Cenozoic eras; includes the Cretaceous, Jurassic, and Triassic periods and is often called the Age of the Reptiles or the Age of the Dinosaurs
Paleozoic geologic era of about 350 million years between the Precambrian and the Mesozoic eras
Permian a geologic period extending from 270 to 220 million years ago
Precambrian name for all geologic time until 600 million years ago; the first living things—algae and bacteria—originated during this time
Tertiary a geologic time period extending from 70 to 1 million years ago
Triassic a geologic period which extends from 225 to 180 million years ago

Dinosaurs and other Mesozoic creatures
Following is a short list of dinosaurs and other animals that coexisted with them. This list contains animals mentioned in this book. In actuality, thousands of different dinosaurs existed. Each year scientists continue to discover remains of new ones.

Allosaurus a carnivore that lived during the Upper (later) Triassic
Apatosaurus, also called *Brontosaurus* a large herbivore that lived in the Upper Jurassic

Brachiosaurus extremely large herbivore with front legs larger than its back ones; lived during the Upper Jurassic
Camptosaurus a small, primitive herbivore which lived in the Upper Jurassic
Compsognathus chicken-sized, this carnivore was one of the smallest and fastest of the dinosaurs; lived in the Mid and Upper Jurassic
Diplodocus at up to ninety feet with its long neck and whip-like tail, this is thought to be the longest dinosaur; a herbivore living in water during the Upper Jurassic
Dromaeosaurus a small Upper Cretaceous carnivore
icthyosaurs large marine animals, not dinosaurs
mosasaurs marine lizards, not dinosaurs
Ornitholestes a small carnivore which lived in the Upper Jurassic
pleiosaurs marine reptiles, not dinosaurs
pterosaurs flying reptiles, not dinosaurs
Stegosaurus large Upper Cretaceous herbivore with a double row of plates along its back
Struthiomimus lightly built carnivore which lived in the Upper Cretaceous; had a bird-like beak and no teeth
Triceratops fierce-looking herbivore with three horns—two over its eyes and one over its snout; lived during the Upper Cretaceous
Tyrannosaurus until recently, thought to be the largest of all land dinosaurs; a carnivore, it weighed eight tons and lived during the Upper Cretaceous
Ultrasaurus recently discovered and the largest dinosaur found up to now

Index

Allosaurus, 22, 23
Alvarez, Luis, 18, 60, 62-66, 67, 70, 81, 84
Alvarez, Walter, 59, 62, 71, 81, 85
Apatosaurus (Brontosaurus), 22, 23, 27, 34

Bakker, Robert T., 22, 35, 39, 41, 84
Brachiosaurus, 22
Brontosaurus
see *Apatosaurus*

Camptosaurus, 22
carnivores, 22, 48
Cenozoic era, 19, 49
Colbert, Edwin H., 43, 49, 65
Compsognathus, 23, 29
continental drift, 22-23, 25, 54
Cretaceous period, 60, 64, 79, 81
Cretaceous-Tertiary boundary, 65, 71
Cuvier, Georges, 13

Dietz, Robert, 63-64
dinosaurs
  definition of, 15
  disappearance of, 29
  see extinction theories
Diplodocus, 22
Dromoaeosaurus, 35

extinction
  time of, 27, 29, 39, 46, 64
extinction theories, 12
  and mammals, 30, 32-33
  asteroids and comets, 10, 60, 62-67, 70-76, 84
    changes in climate, 46-59
    cosmic dust, 76-78
    Nemesis, 67, 70, 73, 74
    Planet X, 74-77
  disease, 38
  drug overdoses, 41

fire, 84
freshwater ocean, 58
greenhouse effect, 50-51, 55
old age, 35-36
random events, 66
small brains, 34
starvation, 43
supernovas, 78-79, 81
volcanoes, 54-55

fossil discoveries, 13
fossil formation, 15, 16, 17, 18, 19

geologic time scale, 19, 20-21
geologists
  definition of, 19
Gould, Stephen Jay, 33, 39, 42, 51

herbivores, 22, 48
Hickey, Leo, 65
Hut, Piet, 70, 74

icthyosaurs, 29, 81
Iguanodon, 14, 25

Kara Crater, 64

Mantell, Gideon, 12-15
Matese, John, 76
McHone, John, 63-64
Mesozoic era, 19, 25-27, 55
  climate, 25-26, 46-59
    Cretaceous period, 19, 25, 27, 46
    Jurassic period, 19, 22, 27
    Triassic period, 19, 25, 34
Meteor Crater, 63
mosasaurs, 29
Muller, Richard, 13, 67, 70, 71, 73, 74, 76

Oort cloud, 70, 76-78
Oort, Jan, 70
Ornitholestes, 23
Owen, Richard, 15

93

paleontologists
  definition of, 16
Paleozoic era, 19
Pangaea, 22-23, 25, 54, 55
Permian period, 34, 66
plesiosaurs, 29, 81
Precambrian era, 19
pterosaurs, 29

Rampino, Michael, 76
Raup, David, 66
Russell, Dale, 58

Sagan, Carl, 72, 86
Sattler, Helen, 35
Sepkoski, John J. Jr., 66, 79
Shlovsky, Iosef, 78

Shoemaker, Eugene, 63, 73
Stegosaurus, 22, 27, 39
Stothers, Richard, 76
Struthiomimus, 35
Swain, Anthony, 41

Tertiary period, 48
Thaddeus, Patrick, 78
Triceratops, 10, 18, 27
twin stars, 67
Tyrannosaurus rex, 18, 23, 27, 39

volcanoes, 54, 55, 66

Whitmire, Daniel, 73, 74, 76

Illustration Credits

Mary Ahrndt, pp. 10, 28, 30, 36, 39, 40, 42, 46, 56, 60, 68, 74, 80, 82, 86.
Michele Mayor Angel, pp. 17, 20, 22, 50, 54.
Culver Pictures, New York, p. 13.
British Museum of Natural History, © DISCOVER MAGAZINE 10-86 Time Inc., p. 14 top.
Courtesy Department of Library Services, American Museum of Natural History: Neg. No. 35608/photo Anderson, p. 14 bottom; Neg. No. 324393, p. 16; Neg. No. 410765, p. 32; Neg. No. 326735, p. 33; Neg. No. 310099/photo E. M. Fulda, p. 35; Neg. No. 36194/photo A.E. Anderson, p. 44; Neg. No. 328655, p. 49; Neg. No. 315110, p. 72; Neg. No. 35422/photo Anderson, p. 78.
Courtesy of University of California Berkeley, Museum of Paleontology, p. 15.
John Sibbick © DISCOVER MAGAZINE 10/86 Time Inc., p. 24. © DISCOVER MAGAZINE 10/86 Time Inc., p. 25.
The Mansell Collection, London, p. 26.
Photo by J. Martin Natvig, University of Colorado Boulder, p. 41.
U.S. Geological Survey: Mt. St. Helens 2, p. 52; R.E. Wallace 191, p. 53; D.R. Roddy, p. 65; E.R. Erdman 220, p. 81.
Wheeler Pictures, New York: © Roger Ressmeyer, pp. 62, 76.
Lick Observatory, University of California Santa Cruz: No. L12, p. 64; No. C21a, p. 67.
Courtesy Daniel P. Whitmire, p. 70.
Copyright 1985 Time Inc. All rights reserved. Reprinted by permission from TIME: pp. 71, 77.

About the Authors

Peter and Connie Roop majored in geology at Lawrence University in Appleton, Wisconsin. Peter, an elementary school teacher, writes historical articles and stories. Connie, a junior high science teacher, serves as a science specialist for *Appraisal* magazine and writes for educational journals. They earned their Masters degrees in Boston and have taught in England.

The Roops have co-authored a dozen books for young people, including *Keep the Lights Burning, Abbie* which was featured on public television's *Reading Rainbow*. They are the authors of three GREAT MYSTERIES: OPPOSING VIEWPOINTS—*Dinosaurs, Poltergeists*, and *The Solar System*.

Peter and Connie live in Appleton, Wisconsin with their children Sterling and Heidi with whom they enjoy traveling, camping, and reading.